BRITAIN
from the air

Introduction

It is very easy to take it for granted that the British Isles are clustered off the edge of north-west Europe and forget how fundamentally this fact has characterised everything about Britain's geography and history.

Despite covering only a small area, Britain features a phenomenal array of landscape and environmental conditions, but escapes the worst extremes the world's weather can offer. Britain has no baking deserts or frozen tundra, nor vast mountain ranges and deep canyons. The British love complaining about the weather but the truth is that the range of temperatures is very limited. It is rarely stiflingly hot in summer, and the winters are relatively mild. There are no tropical storms and hurricane force winds are exceptionally rare. Instead, most of the south and east is fertile agricultural land, and the abundant rivers and streams have made it possible for human beings to have lived in almost every part of Britain since prehistoric times.

Constantly bathed by the Gulf Stream flowing all the way from the Gulf of Mexico, Britain has the great good luck to benefit from the warmth of tropical seas. That way Britain cheats the consequences of a latitude that places it as far north as the much colder Calgary in Canada and Moscow in Russia. Of course it is the sea that defines Britain, just as much as its landscape. The sea provides a natural security, as important in 1940 as it was for thousands of years before. It is a short but dangerous crossing which means nobody has invaded Britain since 1066, but the sea is neither wide enough nor cold enough to prevent people from using it to sail past Britain or to her. So, that way the sea protects Britain but she has never been isolated from the Continent.

It is therefore no surprise that Britain has had the most extraordinarily varied history. Tens of thousands of years ago during the Ice Age men made their way to Britain across the valley where the English Channel is now. By 5,000 years ago, with the ice long gone, the people of the Stone Age were farming and also beginning their great monuments like Avebury. Two and half thousand years ago, Britain's Iron Age tribes were trading with the Continent, including Phoenician traders who came here from the eastern Mediterranean for Cornish tin. In the first century AD, the Roman natural historian Pliny the Elder describes an island off Britain's coast called Mictis where tin was found. That was probably St Michael's Mount in Cornwall. By the time Pliny wrote, the Romans had already invaded, arriving in AD 43. Britain became a Roman province for 360 years, leaving great relics of their presence especially Hadrian's Wall and London.

After the Romans came a succession of new invaders: the Anglo-Saxons from Germany, the Vikings from Denmark and Norway, and then the Normans from Normandy. Each left an indelible stamp on Britain's landscape. The Romans, for example, created the basis of today's road network, while the Normans in 1066 and afterwards built castles and cathedrals that remain amongst the most remarkable monuments in the whole world.

There may have been no invasion since 1066 but Britain's history has guaranteed a constant drama being played out between the British and the land they live in. The Middle Ages saw a continual struggle between the king and his barons, resulting in the castles built almost everywhere from Orford Ness to the coast of Wales. When life became more settled in the sixteenth and seventeenth centuries the rich and powerful found time to build great houses like Longleat and Hatfield.

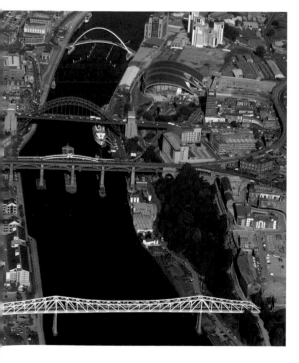

Britain gradually became stronger and stronger until by the dawning of the eighteenth century she had become a world power. It was Britain's Royal Navy and the great seafaring tradition that stretched back over centuries which gave her this colossal advantage. But the most profound impact Britain's new status brought her came in the form of the Industrial Revolution. Until then Britain had always been a rural place – the towns, apart from London, were small and far between. Most of Britain's people lived off the land as they had done from prehistoric times.

By the late 1700s Britain had started to change forever. New industrial towns like Birmingham and Manchester grew where there had been scarcely anything before. Iron ore, coal and water came together to fire the steam engines that drove the mills that grew up in the new towns, supplied by canals carved across the British landscape and the coalmines that gave birth to new towns themselves. Within a few generations, factories, vast chimneys and clouds of smoke became seemingly indelible features of the landscape.

The reason this happened is that Britain is small enough for those essential resources to be brought together when the only power sources available were men and horses. The fact that the stone quarried from the cliffs of the Isle of Purbeck was carried to London and many other places within the British Isles is a reminder that this is a small place. So Britain was the first nation to industrialise, and by the nineteenth century Britain was the most powerful industrialised nation in the world. Her population was growing faster than it had ever done before. What had been only four to five million in medieval times at the most was over nine million by 1801 and had doubled again within 50 years and has tripled from that since then.

During the nineteenth century the railways arrived. The railways did something that was really new. Suddenly men, women and children could travel from one end of Britain to the other quickly and cheaply. It meant not only that towns and cities could grow bigger because workers could commute from further, but it also meant that people could travel from those cities to visit places like the Lake District and the Scottish Highlands, which had once been as remote as the Gobi Desert is to us today. The railways carved their swathes across the landscape, seemingly oblivious to the obstacles in their path. Nothing could stand in their way. Tunnels were built through high ground, and embankments were laid across the Fens. Farm-workers in remote country regions could only look on in amazement as the railways changed their world forever.

No man symbolises the spirit of that age more than Isambard Kingdom Brunel. He built steamships, hacked his way through hills to create tunnels, laid railways and did it all with an unstoppable zeal. It is only appropriate that his Clifton Suspension Bridge still stands today as such a magnificent union of nature and man's industry.

Since those heady days Britain's industrial landscape has changed again. Most of the factories are gone, along with the coalmines. But traces remain everywhere, as do the relics of the most recent great drama Britain experienced: the Second

World War. When Britain faced total defeat in 1940 it might have seemed that all was lost. Air raids led to tens of thousands of casualties, and many of Britain's major towns suffered a great deal of destruction. When the war ended in 1945 Britain faced an uncertain future. Over the next few decades much of her heavy industry disappeared, and a vast amount of urban regeneration followed.

Britain's geographical role today would have been unthinkable to the ancients. She lies midway between Asia and America so that Britain wakes in time to trade with the Far East and is still awake when North America starts its day. The thriving City of London, built on the ruins of the Blitz, makes Britain one of the world's most important financial centres.

No part of Britain's history has escaped being reflected in the landscape visible to us today. It is from the air that this is most apparent and it is a truly wonderful thing to behold. To fly across Britain is to see an endless patchwork of fields, hills, rivers, Iron Age hillforts, Norman castles, villages with their

ancient medieval churches and the cities with their cathedrals and sprawling suburbs. Not everyone has the chance to do that, but in the pages of this book you can see the outstanding beauty of Britain's landscape and also the sheer fascination of seeing the way men and women across the centuries have made this land their own and used it, whether that means admiring the prehistoric people who made Stonehenge or the engineers who built Spaghetti Junction.

But it is also the way to see that however much impact human beings have had on this, one of the most densely populated parts of the world, the natural landscape is still far greater than anything we have done. The epic vistas of the Lake District, the barren ruggedness of Snowdonia, the emotional sight of the white cliffs at Beachy Head and the rolling fields of Worcestershire remind us in the end that Britain is one of the most beautiful and memorable places in the world with more variety and colour than places a hundred times its size.

Scotland

Despite having a population of only a little over five million, Scotland's land area covers the northern third of Great Britain and has played an enormously important role in the history of the British Isles.

Her most distinctive features are the dynamic geology of the Highlands, the lochs, the epic coastline with its endless inlets, the islands scattered around and stretching out in the North Atlantic, and the rolling hills and farmland of the Southern Uplands. It always was a challenging landscape, yet from ancient times tribal peoples braved the elements and made their homes here. The Romans found it impossible to conquer Scotland, and the same challenges faced the invading English kings of the Middle Ages.

It was a curious twist of fate that meant a Scottish king became king of England in 1603 when James VI, Mary Queen of Scots' son, was the only available descendant of Henry VII of England after the death of the childless Elizabeth I. But Scotland remained a separate kingdom until the Act of Union in 1707, though since 1998 devolution has brought Scotland her own parliament once more. Scotland's striking scenery and its remarkable monuments, from castles to the Forth Rail Bridge, make it the perfect place to explore from the air.

OLD MAN OF HOY
Orkney Islands

Hoy is the most south-westerly island in the Orkneys with its sheer west-facing cliffs battered by the Atlantic off Scotland's most northerly tip. Here we are flying north past Hoy's jagged cliffs where far below is the most famous sight in the area: the Old Man of Hoy. The wind, rain and sea have ravaged the sandstone cliffs on their basalt base but this 137-m (450-ft)-high stack has stood firm. First scaled in 1966, it is now an essential challenge for climbers from all round the world.

LISMORE ISLAND
Western Isles

The sun sets over Lismore, a long thin island lying in the Lynn of Lorn just off the coast from Oban in a narrow loch open to the sea. Lismore points to the Island of Mull and its very low-lying land contrasts with the mountains on either side, so it is apt that its Gaelic name means 'great garden'. In AD 592 St Moluag founded a monastery here. Lismore became the seat of the Bishop of Argyll who could sail from here to anywhere.

DUNROBIN CASTLE
Northern Highlands

From this point of view you could easily be forgiven for thinking this is a Bavarian fairytale castle teetering over its terraced gardens with its white stone walls and conical spires, but instead this is the work of Sir Charles Barry, who designed the Houses of Parliament. In the nineteenth century Barry remodelled the medieval castle of the earls of Sutherland and created a 189-roomed castle, said to be the largest in the Highlands, in a unique mix of French Renaissance and Scottish Baronial styles.

RIVER TAY
Southern Highlands

Autumn has just started creeping across the River Tay here as it winds its way across the southern Highlands. The water has the longest journey of any in Scotland, for it fell as rain far to the west in Argyll and Bute and flows 193 km (120 miles) east through Loch Tay and then south to Perth. Here it pours into the North Sea at such a rate that in terms of sheer volume it is the largest river in the British Isles.

EILEAN DONAN CASTLE
Ross-shire

On Scotland's west coast, near Kyle of Lochalsh, three sea lochs (Loch Long, Loch Duich and Loch Alsh) come together at Eilean Donan. Alexander II of Scotland built this castle in the thirteenth century to guard the narrow crossing on the main west coast road. Demolished by the Royal Navy in 1719 after the Spanish captured the castle in support of the Jacobites, Eilean Donan lay in ruins for 200 years until an early twentieth-century restoration, creating a location now popular with film-makers.

INVERNESS
Inverness-shire

Inverness takes its name from the Scottish Gaelic *Inbhir Nis*, meaning 'the mouth of the Ness', a river which flows north-east just a short distance from Loch Ness into the Moray Firth. As such a vital crossing point on Scotland's east coast, it is no wonder that Inverness has been an important place since ancient times and became a royal burgh under William the Lion (1165–1214). Once home to distilling industries, today Inverness is a modern industrial city with a bright outlook.

LOCH LEVEN
Inverness-shire

With an early morning mist swirling above its waters, one would hardly imagine that Loch Leven is now narrowly skirted by the M90 motorway on its way from the Forth Road Bridge north to Perth. Unusually for a Scottish loch, Leven is roughly circular with a 16-km (10-mile) shoreline. Directly below is the thirteenth-century Loch Leven castle on an island, built by the English but later captured by the Scots. The Scottish lords imprisoned Mary Queen of Scots here in 1567.

BEN NEVIS
Inverness-shire

This barren peak is Britain's highest mountain. At just 1,344 m (4,410 ft) Ben Nevis pales into insignificance compared to the Alps or the Rockies, but Scotland is justly proud of this famous place, just a short distance from Fort William. Despite the bleak appearance, Ben Nevis can be walked up by the fit and well-equipped. Thousands of people make it to the top every year. But the mountain is a dangerous place where the weather can turn treacherous in an instant.

GLENDEVON
Perthshire

This is Glendevon, a valley not far from the Firth of Forth on the road south from Auchterarder in Perth and Kinross, and halfway between the city of Perth itself and Stirling. Overlooked by the 485-m (1,590-ft)-high peak of Steel Knowe, and with the gentle undulating Ochil Hills around it, Glendevon is perfect reservoir country, fed by the River Devon. Once this strategic route was controlled by the Douglas family from their castle, but today it is a place for hikers, cyclists and pony trekkers.

DUNNOTTAR CASTLE
Aberdeenshire

Only a mile or so south of Stonehaven on the Aberdeenshire coast facing the North Sea, Dunnottar is the perfect place for a castle. Perched on a rocky outcrop 50 m (164 ft) above the sea, Dunnottar was first fortified at least 2,000 years ago but the present castle dates back to the thirteenth century. Mary Queen of Scots stayed here. It was rebuilt in the seventeenth century to create a luxury castle, but it was largely demolished after the Jacobite rising of 1715 as a punishment.

TROTTERNISH
Isle of Skye

The Isle of Skye is a geologist's dream, and one of its most exciting features is a phenomenal 32-km (20-mile)-long landslip in the Trotternish peninsula at the northernmost end. This is a place of rock, moss and heather, where trees can hardly grow. No wonder climbers and walkers come here to explore the vast rock stacks and pinnacles made of volcanic basalt, braving the 200-m (656-ft) cliffs constantly eroded by the lashing wind and rain in this wild and remote part of Scotland.

SKYE BRIDGE
Isle of Skye

The Skye boat song commemorates romantically how Bonnie Prince Charlie fled to Skye by boat after the defeat of the Jacobite rebellion at Culloden in 1746. Until recently it was still necessary to take a ferry to Skye across the short 500-m (⅓-mile) hop from Kyle of Lochalsh. The controversial toll bridge was opened in 1995 to ease the pressure on ferries as tourism to Skye increased but furious protests about the cost led to the state buying the bridge, and tolls ceased in 2004.

LOCH ETIVE
Argyll and Bute

Loch Etive in Argyll and Bute is a long winding loch fed by the River Etive, fed by water falling on mountains many of which are more than 1,000 m (3,281 ft) high. The loch heads south-west and then makes a sharp turn at Bonawe to head west through a narrow gap at Connal where the waters tumble down the Falls of Lora to meet the sea, about 8 km (5 miles) north of Oban. The contrails in the sky mark the route passenger jets take from London to North America.

LOCH LOMOND
Argyll and Bute

At 37 km (23 miles) long and up to 8 km (5 miles) wide, Loch Lomond has the largest surface area of all of Scotland's lochs though Loch Ness actually has more water in it. Loch Lomond was carved out by glaciers in the Ice Age, and now forms the centrepiece of the Loch Lomond and Trossachs National Park, but is only 22.5 km (14 miles) from Glasgow. Of course it has been immortalised in the famous song with its line 'the bonnie, bonnie banks of Loch Lomond'.

LOCH AWE
Argyll and Bute

At nearly 35 km (22 miles) long, Argyll and Bute's Loch Awe is the longest freshwater loch in Britain, and the third largest. Shaped like a hugely elongated 'y', this is a view of its northern part. Here, overlooked by the mountain of Ben Cruachan, the loch is divided into two by the island of Innis Chonain, now a popular bed-and-breakfast stop on the main road to the coast at Oban. Today the loch is famous for its fishing and the ruined castles perched on several other little islands.

KILCHURN CASTLE
Argyll and Bute

Kilchurn Castle lies at the most northeasterly point of Loch Awe just by the A85 which crosses the Highlands from Perth to Oban. The castle sits by the water's edge on a tiny marshy peninsula and is only easily reached by water. The fifteenth-century castle reached its final form under John, the Earl of Breadalbane in the late 1600s, but was destroyed when a lightning bolt struck it in 1769 and has stood ever since as one of Scotland's most evocative and picturesque ruins.

ST ANDREWS
Fife

The 'Home of Golf', this is St Andrews in Fife on Scotland's east coast overlooking the North Sea. The Society of St Andrews Golfers was founded here in 1754, making it one of the oldest golf clubs in the world. In 1834 the society changed its name to the Royal and Ancient Golf Club of St Andrews when King William IV became its patron. It organises a series of annual championships and dictates the rules of golf all round the globe, except for the United States and Mexico.

FORTH RAIL BRIDGE
Fife

Until the Forth bridges were built, travellers heading north had to take a ferry across the Firth of Forth or head inland to Stirling to cross the river. Between 1883 and 1890 the 2.4-km (1.5-mile)-long Forth Rail Bridge, with its four cantilevers, was built from over 55,000 tons of steel on foundations dug down 27 m (88.5 ft) into the riverbed. It was an epic achievement for the age and is still regarded as one today. The road traffic suspension bridge did not follow until 1964.

STIRLING CASTLE
Stirlingshire

No-one could fail to see the strategic importance of this piece of high ground. This is where the River Forth widens out to make the Firth of Forth. From ancient times it was a vital crossing point on the east coast of Scotland. It was King Alexander I who built the castle here in the early twelfth century, taking advantage of a volcanic outcrop with a sheer drop on three sides. The castle changed hands many times during the wars with the English and was rebuilt in the sixteenth century.

GOUROCK AND RIVER CLYDE
Firth of Clyde

This magnificent view is from high above Gourock and Greenock looking east, on the south side of the Firth of Clyde where the River Clyde flows out to the sea after having passed through Glasgow, just visible in the far distance. In Glasgow's heyday the Clyde was one of the most important rivers for shipbuilding and industry in Britain since it faces west and therefore America. Gourock became a seaside resort for Glasgow's burgeoning population in the late nineteenth century.

CLYDESIDE DOCKS
Glasgow

With Glasgow's greatest days as a shipbuilding centre and port behind her, regeneration of the Clydeside docks is the future. Below to the left are the Yorkhill Quays, built about a century ago where ships bound for America and India set sail, and the SV *Glenlee*, built in Port Glasgow in 1896 and now restored by the Clyde Maritime Trust as one of the nation's core collection of historic ships. Beyond is the Scottish Exhibition and Conference Centre, and to the right the Canting Basin where ships were turned.

EDINBURGH CASTLE
Edinburgh

Princes Street runs through Edinburgh, dividing the Old Town and the New Town, beside the Royal Mile from Holyrood Palace. On the New Town side the street is packed with shops but on the Old Town side there are no buildings, which makes for a marvellous view of Edinburgh Castle, perched on top of the 133-m (436-ft)-high basalt plug of an extinct volcano. As the glaciers retreated at the end of the Ice Age, rubble was trailed behind the basalt plug, creating the Royal Mile.

AILSA CRAIG
Ayrshire

Eighteen km (11 miles) off the South Ayrshire coast from Girvan in the Firth of Clyde, Ailsa Craig is a vast granite volcanic plug that juts out from the sea like the nose of a vast missile. An impressive 338 m (1,110 ft) high, Ailsa's granite was once quarried to make stones for Scotland's traditional sport of curling. In 1833 William Wordsworth wrote a poem about the crag after watching it grow dark during an eclipse of the sun 'towering above the sea and little ships'.

Wales

Wales covers more than 20,720 sq km (8,000 sq miles) and is surrounded by the sea on three sides, making more than 965 km (600 miles) of coastline, despite being no more than 96.5 km (60 miles) wide.

Around three million years ago the Ice Age deepened, and as the ice moved down across the landscape it carved out the mountains and valleys that make Wales so different from the England Midlands to which it joins. The ice only retreated 10,000 years ago, and those hills and valleys became home to ancient prehistoric tribes like the Silures and the Ordovicians who defied the Roman invaders in the first century AD.

Although the Romans conquered Wales the wild landscape never became truly settled and it is little wonder that by the late thirteenth century England's King Edward I had such a struggle to control the Welsh. A massive programme of castle-building brought about the end of Wales's independence. Since then Wales has been ruled along with England but has always retained a powerful sense of its own tradition and history. Welsh, a descendant of the ancient Celtic languages of Europe, is still widely and proudly spoken and today Wales has its own parliament, the Welsh Assembly.

BEAUMARIS CASTLE
Isle of Anglesey

The ultimate textbook castle, Beaumaris was the last castle built in Wales by King Edward I. It was started on the east coast of Anglesey in 1295 to guard the approaches to the Menai Strait (visible in the distance), but before long Edward's attention had turned to Scotland. With neither the money nor the resources to finish it the symmetrical Beaumaris, which means 'the beautiful marshland', was abandoned half-built leaving it a superb example of medieval castle technology at its climax.

MENAI STRAIT
Isle of Anglesey

A real bird's eye view of Thomas Telford's 1826 triumph of engineering in the Industrial Revolution: the Menai Suspension Bridge that joins the island of Anglesey to north-west Wales just by the town of Bangor. At 200 m (656 ft), this is the shortest crossing point in the Strait and might well be the place where the Romans forded across to wipe out a Druid stronghold in the year AD 60. The Druids had been leading the resistance against the Roman invasion.

CAERNARFON
Gwynedd

Here we are flying north-west over Caernarfon in north-west Wales where in the late thirteenth century Edward I built a mighty castle modelled on the walls of Constantinople to guard the Menai Strait. This is where the investiture of the Prince of Wales was held in 1911 and 1969 because the first Prince of Wales, the future Edward II, was born here in 1284. But this is a place where the Welsh identity is at its strongest. Many of the townsfolk speak Welsh.

SNOWDONIA
Gwynedd

Wales's first National Park (created in 1951), Snowdonia, covers over 2,072 sq km (800 sq miles) of epic highland scenery in the principality's north-west. Immensely popular amongst hikers and sightseers alike, the park's centrepiece is Mount Snowdon itself that, despite being 1,085-m (3,560-ft) high, can be reached by taking the Snowdon Mountain Railway. For all its accessibility, Snowdonia is immensely impressive and imposing, a boulder-strewn place of bleak beauty that challenges climbers, especially those who brave the peaks in bad weather, and is one of Britain's wildest places.

PORTMEIRION
Gwynedd

With its Italian Riviera-style architecture, Portmeirion is instantly recognisable as the setting for The Village in the celebrated 1967 television series *The Prisoner*, starring Patrick McGoohan. In reality Portmeirion was designed by Sir Clough Williams-Ellis as a deliberate fantasy place to come and stay. Work started in 1925 and lasted another 50 years, incongruously creating a unique Mediterranean setting on the Welsh coast near Porthmadog. The whole of Portmeirion is a hotel with self-catering houses, but day visitors can explore the place too.

PONTCYSYLLTE AQUEDUCT
Denbighshire

Thomas Telford was one of the inspired men who created great feats of engineering that transformed the British Isles. Canals played a vital part in the Industrial Revolution, transporting raw materials and finished goods. This is the Pontcysyllte Aqueduct, finished in 1805, which carries the Llangollen Canal over the River Dee about 5 km (3 miles) east of Llangollen itself. It took ten years to build the 307-m (1,007-ft)-long aqueduct, using cast-iron to carry the water over masonry arches and piers 38 m (125 ft) above the river below.

BALA LAKE
Gwynedd

The view here is above the town of Bala in Gwynedd looking south-west right down Bala Lake, which is 6.5 km (4 miles) long and 3.3 km (1 mile) wide. It is the largest natural lake in Wales, though it has been made larger as part of local water management systems to control flooding and also the level of the Llangollen Canal. Bala Lake is a very popular place for sailing in the summer months and also boasts the Bala Lake steam railway, which runs along its eastern shore.

HARLECH CASTLE
Gwynedd

Harlech Castle overlooks Tremadog Bay on Wales's west coast and commands the coast road and approaches into Snowdonia. The seaward cliffs made it virtually impregnable and it was cut off from the land by a massive moat and gateway. Like so many Welsh castles, it was built by Edward I in the late thirteenth century. It is no surprise that during the Wars of the Roses Harlech held out for seven years. Supplies arrived by sea and were brought up a narrow cliff staircase to the castle.

CONWY CASTLE

Conwy

Built between 1283 and 1289 by Edward I to control the Conwy estuary and the medieval walled town, Conwy has a long thin layout to fit on the rocky outcrop. Eight massive round towers in the walls surrounding the adjacent inner and outer wards protected the garrison and barbicans reinforced the entrances at either end. Conwy soon fell into disuse apart from a brief revival during the Civil War in the 1640s but remains one of Britain's most impressive castles.

OFFA'S DYKE
Welsh Borders

From ancient times the Welsh Marches saw constant territorial disputes between tribes and later the chieftain kings of the Dark Ages. Offa, Anglo-Saxon King of Mercia (757–96), was one of the most powerful. He ordered the construction of a huge ditch for the western border of his territory with Powys. The Dyke survives to over 20-m (66-ft) wide in places and over 2 m (6.5 ft) in height. One hundred and twelve km (70 miles) of the Dyke can be walked as part of the Offa's Dyke Path National Trail.

PEMBROKESHIRE CASTLE
Pembrokeshire

England's history was made at Pembroke Castle. This was where Henry Tudor grew up, before he defeated Richard III in 1485 and became Henry VII of England. The castle dates back to Norman times but the massive circular keep was built around 1200. Of course it was a perfect place for a castle. The River Cleddau surrounds the site on three sides, and it lies sheltered from Atlantic storms at the eastern end of a bay that stretches west past Milford Haven.

ST DAVID'S
Pembrokeshire

St David's is at almost the most westerly tip of Wales at the very end of St David's peninsula in Pembrokeshire. The city is the smallest in the British Isles, with barely 2,000 inhabitants, and is named after a sixth-century monk born near here who was canonised in 1120. The cathedral was begun about that time and soon became a place of pilgrimage in the Middle Ages. In the foreground here are the ruins of the fourteenth-century bishop's palace.

GOWER PENINSULA
Swansea

The Gower peninsula is on Wales's south coast just a short distance from Swansea and easily reached from the M4. But it remains one of Wales's most outstanding beauty spots, with its 180 sq km (70 sq miles) surrounded on three sides by a coastline with sandy bays used by surfers, such as Oxwich and Port Eynon, the fourteenth-century Weobley Castle, and the small villages scattered across the peninsula. This view is from the north coast across the Llanrhidian Sands towards Llanelli on the mainland.

CATHAYS
Cardiff

Cathays is in the heart of Cardiff, the largest city in the country thanks to the now long-gone coal and steel industries, and capital of Wales since 1955. The building with the tower is Cardiff's city hall, surrounded by other municipal buildings including the crown court and the National Museum of Wales, as well as those belonging to the National Assembly for Wales, created in 1998. Behind is Cathays Park and beyond that is the sprawl of Cardiff University, founded in 1883.

MILLENNIUM STADIUM
Cardiff

For a short while Cardiff's Millennium Stadium held the record for being the largest stadium in the whole of the United Kingdom. It was built in 1999 by the Welsh Rugby Union and can hold nearly 75,000 spectators, as well as having a roof that can be drawn across the pitch to protect it from the rain that Wales knows so well! The pitch itself can be lifted in components so the stadium can be used for non-sporting events like concerts.

CASTELL COCH
Cardiff

Coch is the Welsh word for 'red', so this means 'Red Castle', and of course one can see why. Although there was a castle here for centuries, little was left by the 1800s. The third Marquess of Bute, who also restored Cardiff Castle, decided to rebuild the ruins on the original design as a fantasy castle which appealed hugely to the Victorian love of medieval chivalry and Gothic architecture. The result survives today as a place popular amongst tourists and film producers alike.

BROCKWEIR
Welsh Borders

Here, the River Wye sweeps its way through the magnificent Welsh Borders' countryside, with Wales to the left and England to the right. As the river swings round in a graceful curve, it passes the Glocestershire village of Brockweir, which until 1925 had a thriving shipbuilding industry. Vessels up to 90 tonnes could reach Brockweir from the sea; their cargoes then completed their journeys up the river in shallow barges. The bridge was built in 1906; until then travellers had to cross by ferry.

SEVERN BRIDGES
Severn Estuary

The mighty Severn Estuary was once a barrier between England and South Wales. All traffic had to cross at Gloucester, or take a ferry. The bridge in the distance is the original one, finished in 1966 where the ferry once ran, and now carrying the M48 motorway from Bristol. The bridge in the foreground is just over 5 km (3 miles) in length, and was opened in 1996 to carry the M4. Tolls are charged for crossing into Wales, but the way back is free!

Northern England

Northern England is a proud place, but each of its own regions is prouder still of local traditions and identities.

The landscape is one of rocks, hills, valleys and rivers, with bleak stretches of coastline where places like Scarborough or Bamburgh cling to the rocks on the east. The climax of northern England, though, is probably the Lake District, a place that the Victorians popularised and which remains the region's most famous outdoor destination.

The Romans struggled to tame this part of the province they called Britannia, and their military fortifications are some of the most visible relics of their presence, especially Hadrian's Wall. Later, great medieval cities were founded here to control the roads to the north like Lincoln, York and Durham, where their stupendous cathedrals are amongst the finest examples of medieval architecture in the whole of Europe.

But the north is also where England's Industrial Revolution transformed the country's history and future. Cities like Manchester, Liverpool and Newcastle exploded into prominence during the nineteenth century as centres of industry and trade, with their rivers playing a vital role in their importance. The industry might be largely gone but these places are now undergoing a renaissance, best symbolised by Newcastle's Millennium Bridge and the Imperial War Museum in Salford.

HOLY ISLAND & LINDISFARNE PRIORY

Northumberland

This view is east across the southern part of Holy Island (or Lindisfarne), a tidal island off the Northumberland coast only accessible by road during low tide. In the foreground is the monastery, founded by St Aidan in the seventh century, where some of the most important and famous illuminated Biblical manuscripts were created by the monks. After the Dissolution of the Monasteries under Henry VIII, the buildings were robbed to build the castle in the distance, later remodelled by Sir Edwin Lutyens.

BAMBURGH CASTLE

Northumberland

The mighty castle at Bamburgh on Northumberland's coast owes its importance to the basalt outcrop on which it was built by Henry II in the twelfth century, from where it commands views in every direction. Three hundred years later Henry VI made Bamburgh his base during the Wars of the Roses, but the castle fell to one of the first uses of gunpowder in England when Edward IV attacked it. The castle would have remained in ruins had it not been for a late Victorian restoration.

HADRIAN'S WALL
Northumberland

When the Romans built their Wall in northern Britain as a frontier in the AD 120s, on the orders of the emperor Hadrian, they took advantage of every natural feature. Here the Wall, roughly halfway along its 122 km (76 mile) course, hugs the top of steep north-facing crags. In the foreground is one of the miniature forts built every mile along the Wall. A small band of troops was billeted in each one to guard this bleak outpost of the Roman Empire.

CHESTERS
Northumberland

The foundations visible here are some of the buildings belonging to the Roman fort of Cilurnum (Chesters) on Hadrian's Wall, built about the year AD 125 and home to a unit of cavalry who guarded this crossing on the River Tyne. The land was owned in the nineteenth century by an antiquarian called John Clayton who loved the Wall and its monuments. He turned the fort ruins into a country park and built a museum, which are today in the care of English Heritage.

ANGEL OF THE NORTH
Gateshead

This is where the A167 to Gateshead parts company with the A1, which takes through traffic past the west of Newcastle-upon-Tyne. Travellers heading north are greeted by the enormous steel Angel of the North, commissioned by Gateshead Council and designed by Anthony Gormley. She has overlooked the junction with her 54-m (177-ft)-wide wings since 1998. The curious and distinctive colour was created by mixing copper with 200 tons of steel, which oxidised. Not surprisingly, the sculpture has both fans and critics.

TYNE BRIDGES
Gateshead

The River Tyne is the soul of Newcastle and also the driving force behind its growth in the Industrial Revolution. Bridges over the river have played a vital role in the city's history – the Romans built the first one here in about AD 125. The bridge in the middle, known as the 'High Level Bridge', was built by Robert Stephenson in 1849 to carry a road and railway. The one beyond is the Tyne Bridge, built in 1928 and based on Sydney Harbour Bridge in Australia.

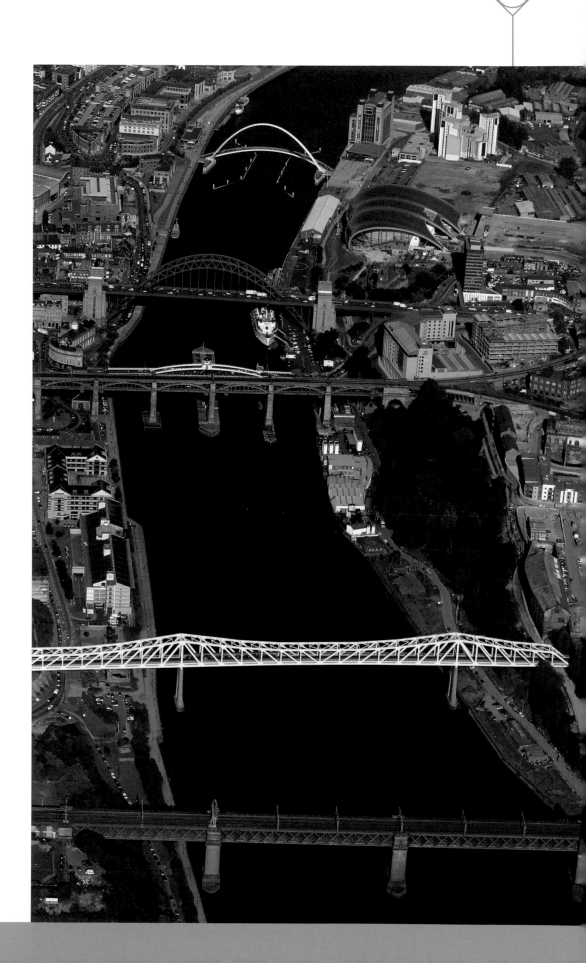

BRIMHAM ROCKS
North Yorkshire

This is Brimham in Nidderdale in the heart of Yorkshire, west of Harrogate and Ripon. Millions of years ago this was a river delta, where the water deposited the granite and silt it had carried down from mountains to the north, creating a hard sandstone known as millstone grit. At the end of the Ice Age 10,000 years ago, the rock was exposed to the wind and rain, creating a spectacular series of eroded formations known today as Brimham Rocks.

ROBIN HOOD'S BAY
North Yorkshire

Robin Hood's Bay is where the York Moors National Park meets the sea near Whitby, though there is no known connection with Robin Hood. The little village, also known as Robin Hood's Bay, is these days a place for holidaymakers, with camping and caravan parks dotted round about, offering everything from visits to the old coastguard station and pony-trekking to fossil hunting along the cliffs. In time gone by this was a fishing village, with a reputation for smuggling.

SCARBOROUGH
North Yorkshire

Scarborough is Yorkshire's most famous seaside resort and lies on the coast where the Vikings founded it in the tenth century. The twelfth-century castle is the most prominent feature in this view, and rightly so since it sits on top of a headland nearly 100 m (328 ft) high. Eight hundred years before, the Romans built a signal station here to protect their coastal shipping. Scarborough today is a major town with a Victorian promenade, the Stephen Joseph Theatre, and also hosts a jazz festival.

CASTLE HOWARD
North Yorkshire

Castle Howard is one of the glories of Yorkshire, sitting within its vast gardens a few miles north of York. Built by John Vanbrugh and Nicholas Hawksmoor for the Earl of Carlisle at the beginning of the eighteenth century, it is really a magnificent country pile rather than a castle. This view is from behind the house looking across the formal garden. It is hard to believe a fire in 1940 devastated Castle Howard because since then the building has been entirely restored.

YORK MINSTER
North Yorkshire

Mighty York Minster is England's largest cathedral, and still towers over the largely medieval streets that cluster round below, including the famous Shambles. Once known as Eboracum, York began life as a Roman fortress, remains of which can be seen beneath the Minster. The present church dates back to the eleventh century but repairs and alterations ended up creating one of the greatest Gothic twelfth-century buildings ever created, though work carried on until 1472. A terrible fire wrecked the south transept in 1984, which has since been restored.

BLACKPOOL
Lancashire

There is no doubt that this is England's most famous seaside view. On the Lancashire coast, Blackpool has three piers built by the Victorians, but in 1894 its most distinctive feature was built: Blackpool Tower. Blackpool's greatest days came in the twentieth century when working-class people arrived in their tens of thousands every week during the summer season from all round the country. Blackpool remains an important leisure destination and also plays host to party political conferences and many other events.

IMPERIAL WAR MUSEUM NORTH

Manchester

This extraordinary piece of engineering is the Imperial War Museum North in Salford, Manchester. The building was designed with aluminium as an outer skin by the Berlin-based American architect Daniel Libeskind to be a symbol of world war by creating a series of conflicting shapes and angles. The view shows the museum under construction before opening in 2002 in The Quays, Manchester's cultural and leisure centre that includes shopping, watersports and other museums. The ship at lower right is the minesweeper HMS *Bronington*.

MERSEY ESTUARY

Liverpool

Few cities in England have as much civic pride and identity as Liverpool, seen here from above the Mersey Estuary. Liverpool grew to colossal commercial importance in the eighteenth century as the British Empire became more and more powerful. By the early 1800s nearly half the world's trade passed through Liverpool. It remains an important port today though its greatest modern fame has come from the association with popular music in the 1960s, mainly of course due to the Beatles.

MANCHESTER SHIP CANAL

Manchester

A ship makes its way up the 58-km (36-mile)-long Manchester Ship Canal. Starting at Runcorn on the south side of the Mersey Estuary, the canal was finished on 1 January 1894, having taken six years to build. During its constrcution, as many as 17,000 men removed 41 million cubic m (54 million cubic yds) of spoil. The reason for this Herculean effort was to provide Manchester with its own access to the sea and end its dependence on nearby Liverpool.

CHESTER
Cheshire

Chester was once Roman Deva, founded by the River Dee as the fortress of the Twentieth legion to control northern Wales. Within the ancient walls, though, Chester's proudest boasts are its thirteenth-century cathedral with its freestanding bell tower built in 1974, and its magnificent half-timbered buildings with their unique double-rows or 'galleries' of shops, making this one of England's best-preserved medieval cities. Although the Victorians added Gothic buildings like the town hall, they also replicated the medieval style, helping to preserve Chester's character.

CHOLMONDELEY CASTLE
Cheshire

Cholmondeley Castle is near Malpas in Cheshire. Cholmondeley looks medieval but in reality was built in the nineteenth century as a mock castle, a time when many people loved the idea of medieval life and tried to recreate it. Cholmondeley's fame, though, belongs to its magnificent gardens surrounding the house, which overlooks a lake. As well as a water and a rose garden, Cholmondeley has plenty of full-grown trees, many of which can be seen here clustering around the house.

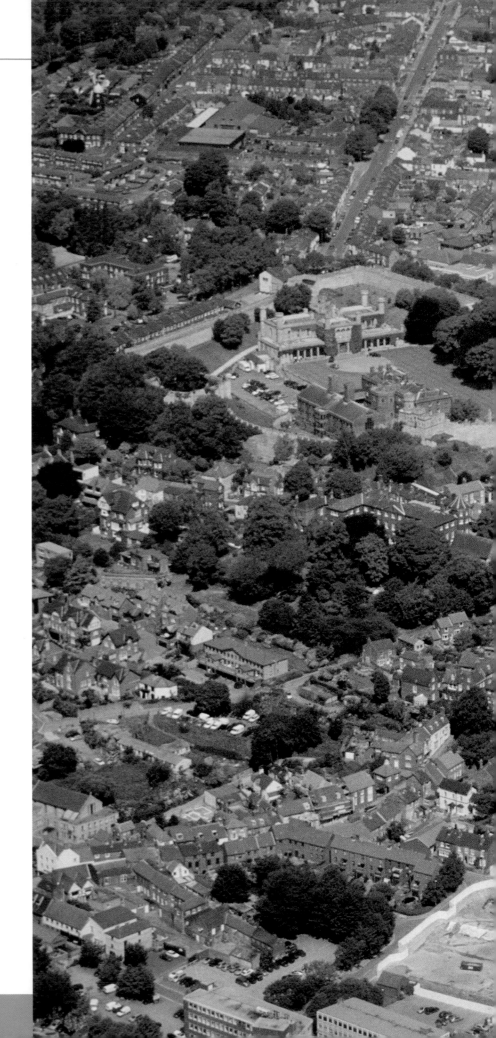

LINCOLN CATHEDRAL

Lincolnshire

No other English cathedral dominates its surroundings like Lincoln. Lincoln Cathedral was begun by the Normans in 1072 in the middle of the upper town, on a hill which towers over the lower town and the surrounding flat Lincolnshire farmland. No wonder the site was earlier a Roman legionary fortress. The cathedral was destroyed by fire and an earthquake before the end of the 1100s and most of the present building belongs to the thirteenth century. Lincoln's 83-m (272-ft)-high tower commands staggering views across the county.

Heart of England

The Heart of England is a vast area that stretches from the River Trent in the east to the River Severn in the west.

A wonderfully varied landscape, so often crossed by travellers hurrying from London to the north or vice-versa, this is a region without the extremes of the north and west but with its own beauty and endless range of fascinating places. It enjoys the advantages of being close to the crowded south-east, as well as the luxury of its own cities and towns like Stratford and Cheltenham, and parks.

The natural landscape includes the Peak District National Park, which is probably the most unspoiled part of the region, as well as the rolling Cotswolds. In the Middle Ages castles ruled this part of England as they did everywhere else, but by the sixteenth and seventeenth centuries stately homes had replaced them as places for the rich and influential to demonstrate their power, resulting in spectacular houses like Chatsworth and Blenheim.

But the heart of England was also home to the Industrial Revolution, with Ironbridge setting the trend for the future as far back as the late eighteenth century. More recently Leicester's Space Centre and Alton Towers place the region firmly in the present.

PEAK DISTRICT
Derbyshire

An early morning mist waits to burn off in the Peak District National Park, an area bounded by Manchester, Huddersfield, Sheffield and Matlock in the centre of England. Apart from Buxton there are no towns, only villages, in the park which is bisected by the River Derwent. The Peaks are popular for day trippers from the towns around, with some people coming to walk while the more ambitious go climbing on rocks like the gritstone Stanage, or caving underneath the White Peak.

HARDWICK HALL
Derbyshire

Bess of Hardwick was one of the richest women in Elizabethan England, and she used her wealth to build this spectacular showcase of Tudor ostentation near Chesterfield in the late sixteenth century. The huge windows, easily visible even from this height, were a way of showing off Bess's extravagance, as were her monogrammed initials 'ES' displayed along the roof line. The house survives more or less as it was built, together with its ornamental gardens, and is now owned by the National Trust.

CHATSWORTH HOUSE
Derbyshire

Chatsworth, a few miles from Bakewell in Derbyshire, is home to the dukes of Devonshire. The Tudor house was completely remodelled in the 1600s by the first duke. Like so many great houses, Chatsworth faced ruin in the twentieth century with the upheaval of war, death duties and the astronomical running costs. But by turning the house into a charitable trust, the family reinvented Chatsworth and it is now one of the most successful and popular stately homes in England.

DOVEDALE
Derbyshire/Staffordshire

The River Dove drains the gritstone moor from Axe Edge in the south-west part of the Peak District National Park, bounded by Ashbourne, Leek and Buxton, and marks the line between Derbyshire and Staffordshire. The river, responsible for cutting through the limestone to create remarkable rock formations, has also been famous for trout-fishing for centuries, immortalised by Izaak Walton in his *The Compleat Angler* (1653). Now known as Dovedale, and owned by the National Trust, the area is one of the most beautiful in England.

KERSALL

Nottinghamshire

This might be almost any part of rural England with an endless patchwork quilt of fields. In fact this is late one autumn afternoon at a tiny village called Kersall, halfway between Sherwood Forest and Newark in Nottinghamshire and connected by the A616, visible in the middle distance. Far beyond at the upper right is the power station at Cottam. It sits by the great River Trent, which has made this such a fertile place for farmers since ancient times.

SHERWOOD FOREST

Nottinghamshire

Sherwood near Edinstowe in Nottinghamshire was once a royal forest but is now a park with a visitor centre and tourist attractions. No-one can hear the name 'Sherwood Forest' without thinking of the legendary Robin Hood of Sherwood, who reputedly defended the downtrodden during the time Prince John ruled England while his brother, Richard I (1189–99), was away on the Crusades and imprisoned in Austria. Deep in its heart is the ancient 1,000-year-old 'Major Oak', said to have been Robin's headquarters.

INNER-CITY HOUSING
Nottingham

Inner-city housing is a necessary evil and goes all the way back to the Industrial Revolution when the rural population started heading to the towns looking for work in the new factories. Ever since then, Britain's cities and towns have grown bigger and bigger and now most of us live in one. These houses were built around the end of the nineteenth century to take advantage of railway commuter lines, and still form part of essential housing stock in all of Britain's major conurbations.

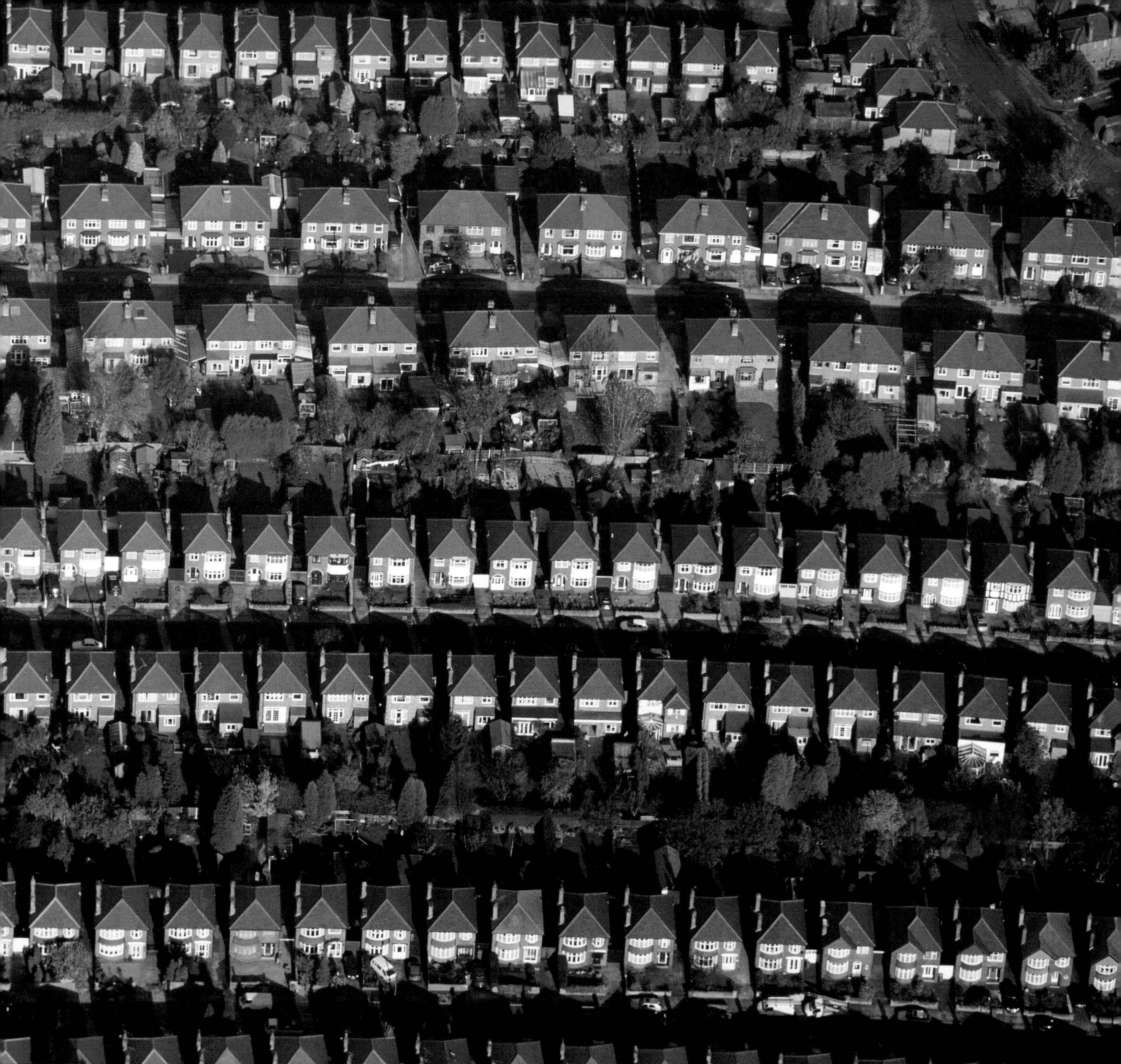

ALTON TOWERS

Staffordshire

From up here, Alton Towers' Corkscrew ride looks fairly harmless but this is the theme park's original roller-coaster, built here in 1980. Alton Towers is England's biggest and best-known theme park, built around the nineteenth-century Alton Towers mansion in Staffordshire. Alton Towers is known today for its terrifying and eye-watering rides like Nemesis and Oblivion, which plunges riders deep below the ground in a vertical drop. But Alton Towers also has plenty of other gentler activities, including a petting zoo.

NATIONAL SPACE CENTRE
Leicestershire

Leicester is one of the most important Midlands cities. One of its latest and proudest boasts is the futuristic National Space Centre with its Rocket Tower visible here beside the museum building. It is the only such place devoted to the history and future of space exploration of the Earth and Moon, the planets and beyond the Solar System in the United Kingdom. Visitors can explore Jupiter's ice-bound moon Europa and tour a lunar base set in the year 2025.

RIVER SEVERN
Shropshire

At about 354 km (220 miles) long the Severn is the longest river in the British Isles with the greatest water flow, helped by the Avon and the Wye that pour into it. The Severn flows out into the Bristol Channel after having passed through Shrewsbury, Worcester and Gloucester since it rose in Wales. Thanks to a 15-m (492-ft) tidal range, its most remarkable phenomenon is the Severn Bore caused by exceptional high tides pushing back up the estuary against the river to create a wave.

IRONBRIDGE GORGE
Shropshire

In the upper reaches of the River Severn is the Ironbridge Gorge in Shropshire, a place enshrined in history as the 'birthplace of the Industrial Revolution' because this was where Abraham Darby found the most effective way to smelt iron with coke in 1709. Appropriately enough, the most famous monument here is the Ironbridge itself, constructed from 800 separate cast iron parts by Darby's grandson, also Abraham, in 1779. Although small by modern standards, Ironbridge was a momentous achievement that changed the course of history.

HILL CROOME
Worcestershire

The heart of the rolling Worcestershire countryside seems totally at peace here, in spite of the fact that this is Hill Croome, a tiny hamlet just yards from the busy M5 motorway that carries traffic from the West Midlands to Bristol and the south-west. Although the county is mainly rural, Worcesteshire's most famous product is Worcestershire Sauce, made in the cathedral city of Worcester from (amongst other things), vinegar, molasses, onion, garlic, and anchovies and used throughout the world.

GRAND UNION CANAL
Birmingham

Begun in the 1760s, the canals helped the Industrial Revolution get underway by making it possible to move the resources needed to smelt iron to the same place, and to ship out the products of industry. But the result was also to create the railways and road transport. By the early twentieth century canals faced ruin, so a scheme was devised to join canals together and create a single 217-km (135-mile) canal link with 160 locks to connect London and Birmingham, which remains in use today.

SPAGHETTI JUNCTION
Birmingham

It was the Industrial Revolution that turned a cluster of villages in the West Midlands into England's second city. Road development in the twentieth century, especially motorways, made Birmingham into a major junction. That resulted in what was seen by many as a symbol of how Britain was sacrificing the environment to the car, and by others as a necessary evil: Spaghetti Junction, built from 1968–72. Its real name is Gravelly Hill interchange on the M6 and it covers an amazing 12 ha (30 acres).

UNIVERSITY OF BIRMINGHAM
Birmingham

With around 25,000 students, Birmingham University is one of the largest in Britain. The university was awarded its charter in 1900, and the red brick of its buildings visible here happily echoes the fact that this was the first of the modern era of so-called 'red-brick universities' to achieve that status. This view shows the D-shaped design of its Edgbaston campus, designed by the architects Aston Webb and Ingress Bell, around the Chamberlain clock tower which rises to 100 m (328 ft).

WEOLEY CASTLE

Birmingham

Today Weoley Castle is a south-west suburb of Birmingham, but it takes its name from the fortified medieval manor house of that name whose ruins are still visible. Weoley reached its climax in the fifteenth century and it is almost impossible to believe now that it was once surrounded by its own 121 ha (300 acres) of farmland. Soon afterwards it changed hands and fell into ruin only to be swamped as Birmingham swallowed up surrounding countryside in the nineteenth century to become England's second biggest city.

GOODRICH CASTLE

Herefordshire

Goodrich's red sandstone walls mirror the Herefordshire farmland that surrounds this massive stronghold built near Ross-on-Wye by Godric Mappeston in the twelfth century. The earls of Pembroke enlarged and strengthened the castle, cutting the rock out from around the castle to create the moat at the same time. The abandoned castle was used by both sides in the English Civil War and was later partly demolished to prevent it being of further use, but as one can see the castle resisted well.

WARWICK CASTLE
Warwickshire

Warwick is an exceptionally magnificent medieval castle with a splendid history stretching all the way back to William the Conqueror, though it did not reach its present form until the late fourteenth century. It remained in the hands of several different families, each successively different creations of the earls of Warwick until, in 1978, it was bought by the Tussauds Group. The group turned it into a major medieval heritage centre where visitors can watch medieval siege warfare machines and the training of birds of prey.

STRATFORD-ON-AVON
Warwickshire

Stratford-on-Avon is an international shrine to William Shakespeare, born here in 1564, though he spent much of his life writing and performing in London. This prominent building is the Royal Shakespeare Theatre where the playwright's works are constantly performed to audiences who have travelled here from every part of the world. Built in 1933, it can seat around 1,500 people. Stratford also boasts Shakespeare's birthplace, and the house of his wife Anne Hathaway. From here the Avon flows south-west to join the Severn at Tewkesbury.

TEWKESBURY
Gloucestershire

Tewkesbury stands where the River Avon meets the Severn and was where, in 1471, the Wars of the Roses ended in a battle between Edward IV and the supporters of Henry VI. The last bloody moments took place in Tewkesbury's Abbey of the Blessed Virgin Mary, the town's greatest building, built in the twelfth century from Normandy Caen stone shipped up the Severn. The church survived Henry VIII's Dissolution of the Monasteries and is today England's second largest parish church.

SUDELEY CASTLE
Gloucestershire

Sudeley, near Winchcombe in the Gloucestershire Cotswolds, is the burial place of a queen. Katherine Parr, the last of Henry VIII's six wives is buried in the chapel here. After the king's death she married Thomas Seymour, whose home this was, and died in 1548. Sudeley fell into ruin after it was used as Prince Rupert's headquarters in the Civil War, but a massive restoration programme began in the nineteenth century when the Dent family, still the owners, bought the castle.

CHELTENHAM
Gloucestershire

Cheltenham was just another market town until healing waters were found nearby in 1716. In 1788 George III came to 'take the waters' and promptly made Cheltenham into the height of fashion. Over the next few decades several spas were set up and embellished with the fine architecture that now makes Cheltenham England's most complete Regency town. One of the finest is the Queen's Hotel, claimed to be the nation's first purpose-built hotel, seen here looking down Cheltenham's tree-lined promenade.

COTSWOLDS
Gloucestershire/Oxfordshire

The rolling hills of the Cotswolds lie south of Oxford and were formed from limestone that was once a seabed in the Jurassic age and is made from the bodies of untold billions of sea creatures. The stone is wonderfully easy to carve when freshly quarried, and weathers into a gentle range of brown and grey shades that make the Cotswold villages so charming. Despite its proximity to London and motorways, it remains a perfect piece of quintessential English countryside.

BLENHEIM PALACE
Oxfordshire

This breathtaking building near Woodstock in Oxfordshire was built on a site awarded to John Churchill, Duke of Marlborough, by Queen Anne as a gift for defeating the French at Blenheim in 1704. Designed by Sir John Vanbrugh and built from 1705–22, Blenheim is the only house known as a 'palace' that is neither a royal nor a bishop's residence. Blenheim has remained in the Churchill family. Sir Winston Churchill was born here in 1874 when his mother was attending a ball.

OXFORD
Oxfordshire

At the heart of this view of the city is Christ Church College, originally founded as Cardinal's College in 1524. Henry VIII re-founded the college as Christ Church in 1546. In 1682, Christopher Wren, an alumni, designed a tower to house the college's bell, 'Great Tom', from which the quadrangle and the tower get their names. The university so dominates the city that it is easy to forget that until the 1970s Oxford was also a major car-manufacturing centre.

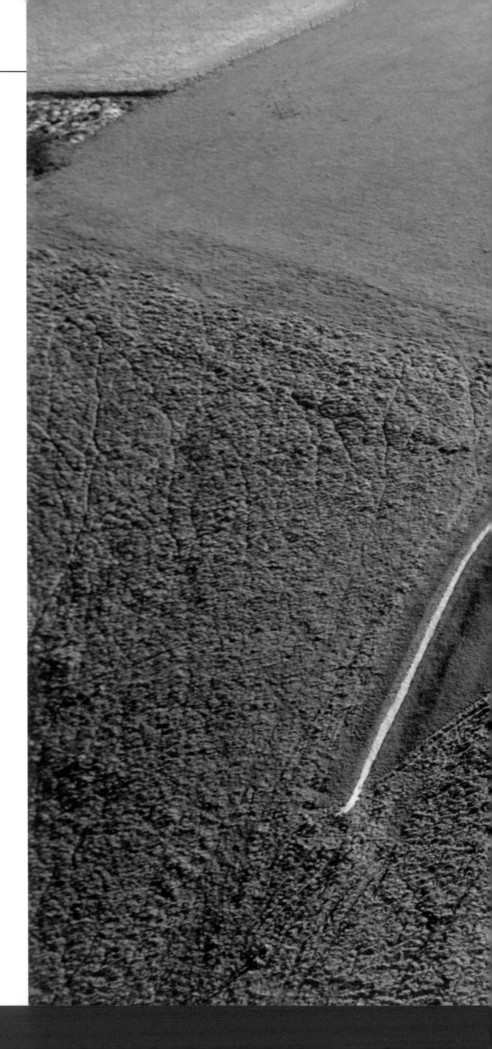

UFFINGTON WHITE HORSE
Oxfordshire

No-one knows who created the White Horse by exposing the chalk beneath on the Ridgeway across the Lambourn Downs, or why – since the only place to see it properly is from the air. But the 110-m (360-ft)-wide figure dates back at least to 600 BC and possibly before, created by the prehistoric peoples who were responsible for so many monuments in this ancient part of Britain. On the ground the horse is best seen from the north, appropriately across the Vale of White Horse.

Eastern England

Eastern England is East Anglia, named after the Angles who arrived here from northern Europe in the fifth century.

As a landscape its most defining feature is the flatness creating a part of Britain where the 'big sky' is always in evidence, whether one is exploring Cambridge's ancient medieval streets or enjoying a gentle cruise down one of the Norfolk Broads.

East Anglia is not a region where heavy industry has ever really had much of a presence, and instead it retains much of its traditional character as a place of peaceful agriculture and where man is constantly challenged by the need to control water in all its forms. In the Middle Ages this was an exceptionally rich part of Britain, thanks to the trade in wool, and some of the finest architecture in the country can be seen here in cities that are today far less important than they once were, such as Ely.

But East Anglia features strongly in the romantic sensibilities of the English, epitomised by the poetry of John Clare and the paintings of John Constable. Its proximity to the south-east has guaranteed its popularity as a holiday and weekend destination for those desperate to escape London.

SANDRINGHAM HOUSE
Norfolk

Sandringham was built in the 1770s in the middle of 3,238 ha (8,000 acres) of Norfolk countryside, and bought in 1862 by Queen Victoria for her son, the future Edward VII. Edward found the house too small, so in the 1870s he replaced it with the present house. This was where King George V died in 1952, and today's royal family spend the first part of each year here to commemorate that, though at other times the house is open to the public.

BRANCASTER HARBOUR
Norfolk

Brancaster is one of the most remote and unspoiled parts of East Anglia. It lies on the north-west coast of Norfolk and enjoys a spectacular view across the North Sea and the entrance to the Wash, the vast marshy inlet that separates Norfolk from Lincolnshire. Once the site of the Roman fort of Branodunum, traces of which are still visible, Brancaster is now an important refuge for wildlife, especially birds. The wide sandy beaches attract holidaymakers, and the offshore wind sailing enthusiasts.

HOLKHAM BEACH
Norfolk

Holkham faces out towards the North Sea in this view looking east across the flat north Norfolk coastline between Wells-next-the-Sea and Burnham Market. The wide sandy beaches in this quiet and remote part of England make the region a popular holiday destination. Walkers also enjoy this part of the world because the Peddars Way and Norfolk Coast Path makes its way along the shoreline here, shielded from the weather by the prominent band of trees known as Holkham Pines.

LOWESTOFT HARBOUR
Norfolk

The view here is across the south pier and outer harbour; beyond are the docks and north Lowestoft, the town's commercial district. Lowestoft is one of Norfolk's two major east coast ports, the other (and Lowestoft's rival) being Great Yarmouth. Both grew in importance during the Middle Ages on the back of the fishing industry, but in recent times Lowestoft has benefited enormously from servicing the North Sea oil and gas rigs, as well as from tourism.

HICKLING BROAD
Norfolk

This is not the sea but one of the Norfolk Broads. Hickling is one of several broads between Norwich and the sea. The story of Eastern England has always been one about water and the battle to control it. The endless low-lying land is constantly susceptible to storms bringing high sea levels, and the rivers can easily flood. But the water also provides the region with a source of beauty, defining the landscape with the marshy fens and the Norfolk Broads.

ELY CATHEDRAL

Cambridgeshire

In the heart of the Cambridgeshire Fens by the River Great Ouse sits the small town of Ely, dwarfed by its magnificent cathedral, visible for miles across the flatlands of eastern England. A Saxon monastery was founded here in AD 673, but the present cathedral was begun in the late eleventh century. In 1322 the tower collapsed and in its place a unique octagonal Gothic dome was built. By the fifteenth century the north-west transept had collapsed, too, but has never been replaced.

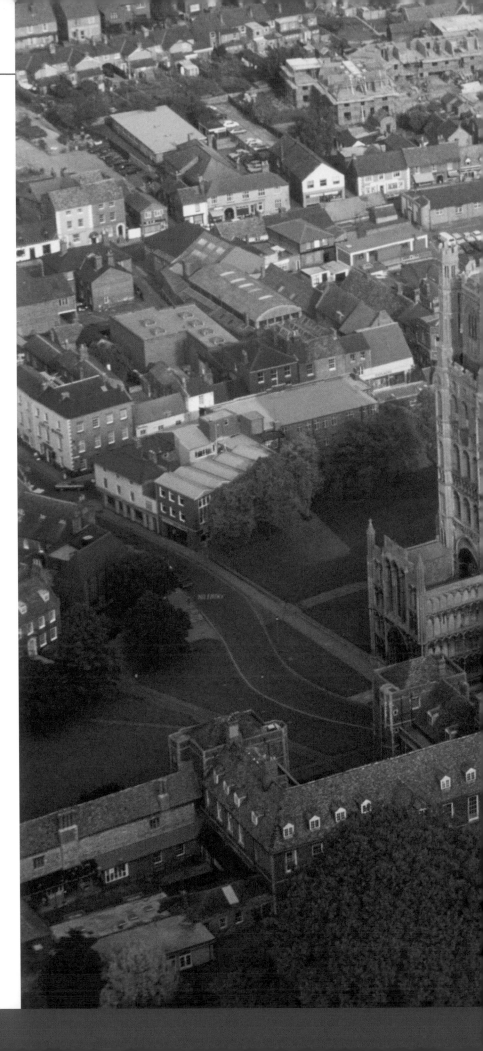

CAMBRIDGE
Cambridgeshire

Cambridge is England's 'other' ancient university city, the university being founded by students from Oxford who fled here in the early 1200s. Today Cambridge is still dominated by the colleges, and especially by the fifteenth-century King's College Chapel. But the university is only half the story today. Cambridge is a high-tech city with a thriving population and excellent transport links to London, just 80 km (50 miles) away. As a result it has become one of the most expensive places to live in England.

ALTHORP
Northamptonshire

Until 1981 it is unlikely that many people had ever heard of Althorp near Northampton, the family home of the earls of Spencer. It was the marriage of Lady Diana Spencer to the Prince of Wales which brought the house, pronounced 'All-trop', to wider attention. Althorp has been owned by the Spencers since the sixteenth century. Today the house can be visited by the public, many of whom come to see where Diana was buried on an island in the lake in 1997.

TULIPS
East Anglia

This looks almost like a colour test chart, though in fact it is a field of tulips in East Anglia. Tulips were brought to Europe, probably from Turkey, in the sixteenth century and soon became extremely popular, especially in the Netherlands where many new varieties were cultivated. The rich dark soils of East Anglia's fens are perfect for tulip-growing, and these days the region is the centre of Britain's flower-growing industry, celebrated with various festivals including the flower parade in Spalding, Lincolnshire.

SNAPE MUDFLATS
Suffolk

In this mid-morning view, Snape's mudlflats look like polished bronze. This is where the River Alde winds its way east only to turn abruptly south just before it reaches the Suffolk coast, and carries on for another 17 km (10 miles) before finally flowing into the North Sea. These waters once carried Snape's malted barley by barge all the way to London where it was brewed into beer. The preserved buildings of the maltings now play host to part of the annual Aldeburgh Music Festival.

ORFORD CASTLE

Suffolk

This is Orford Ness, not far north of Felixstowe on the
Suffolk coast, overlooked by Henry II's unusual castle and in
the far distance the lighthouse. Orford Castle was built in the
mid 1160s to give Henry a foothold in a land ruled by barons
who he needed to control. This views shows off the castle's
radical polygonal design that gave it 21 sides and three
towers. Today the village clusters around the motte but once
there were other castle buildings, now long demolished.

KENTWELL HALL

Suffolk

In the Middle Ages Suffolk's wealth came from wool, and
the Clopton family did especially well out of it. The result
was one of England's finest Tudor manor houses, close to
the village of Long Melford, built in the early 1500s. Castles
were really a thing of the past but old habits die hard and
Kentwell was surrounded by a moat. Today Kentwell
boasts a working Tudor kitchen and is a living history
centre, hosting re-enactments of Tudor life and even
Second World War events.

AUDLEY END HOUSE
Essex

This is Audley End House in the heart of Essex with Saffron Walden visible beyond. If the early seventeenth-century house, built on the site of a Benedictine monastery, looks impressive enough today it is remarkable to discover that it was once a very great deal larger. Thomas Howard, Earl of Suffolk, built Audley at colossal expense to impress King James I. But over the next two centuries various parts of the sprawling pile were demolished to make the place manageable.

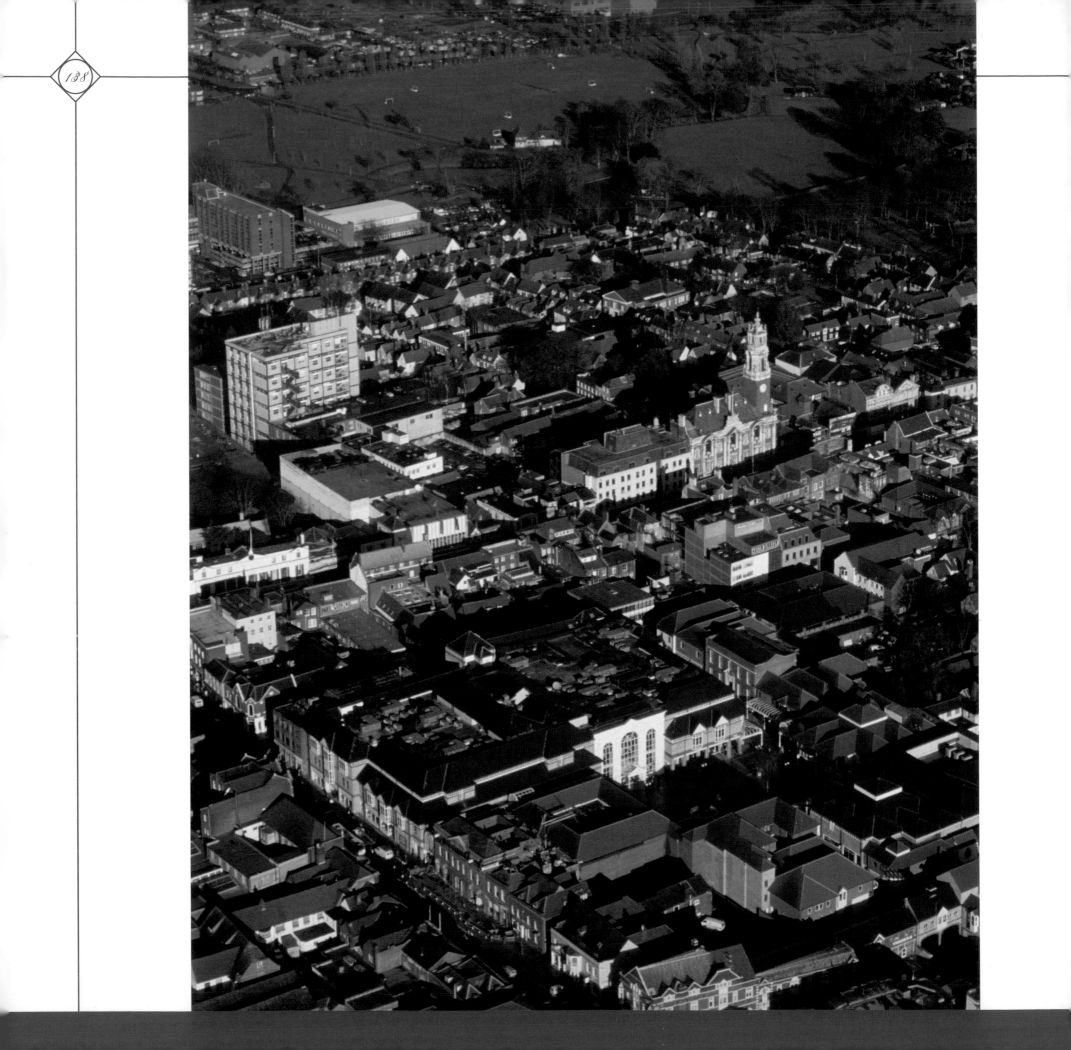

COLCHESTER
Essex

Colchester can justly claim to be the oldest town in Britain. In the Iron Age this was Camulodunum, capital of the Catuvellauni from where Cunobelinus ruled most of Essex and Hertfordshire. The Romans arrived in AD 43, and Camulodunum became first a legionary fortress and then a proper Roman town with a senate house, theatre and a massive temple. Today Colchester has outgrown its Roman walls, but its ancient traditions are proudly displayed to visitors in the castle, which stands on top of the temple's foundations.

TILBURY FORT
Essex

The idea behind Tilbury's diamond-shaped projecting bastions was to make sure the fort's defenders could cover every possible angle against an artillery attack from enemy ships. The fort was a vital defence against a naval attack up the Thames to London, made all the more urgent because in 1667 the Dutch Navy had attacked the Medway and seized some of England's capital ships. Tilbury was begun 1672 by Charles II and it guarded the Thames until as recently as 1950.

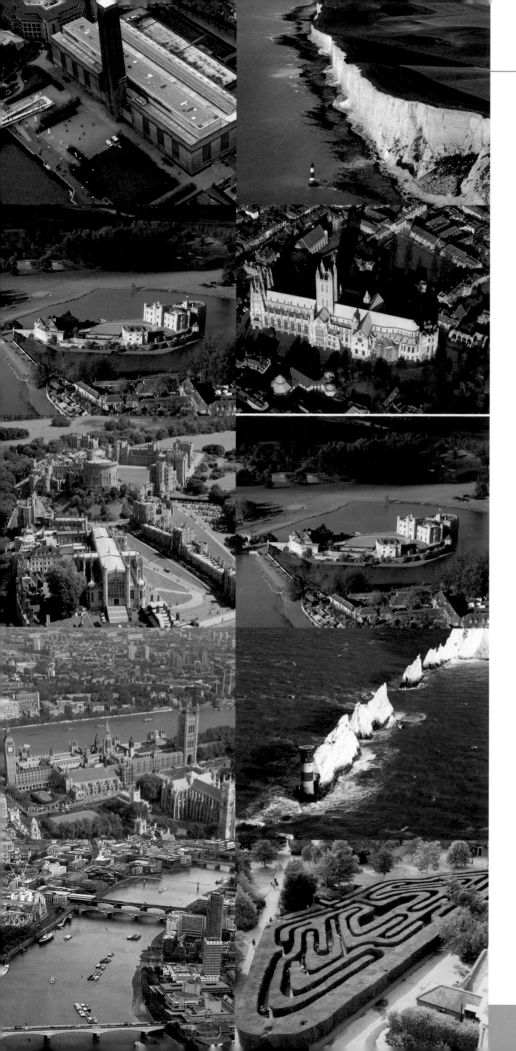

South-East England

South-east England is the busiest and most crowded part of the whole British Isles. Inevitably it is dominated by the all-consuming sprawl of London, one of the world's greatest cities and certainly one of the most interesting.

With a history stretching back to Roman times, London became the largest medieval city in the country and by the seventeenth century dwarfed every other town in Britain and most of those in Europe. The Thames is the life-force of London and it deserves to be viewed from every angle, including during the annual London Marathon when tens of thousands of runners make their way through the middle of the capital.

But there is far more to the south-east than just London. Like so many other parts of Britain, castles stand as witness to the turbulent years of the Middle Ages and cathedrals like Chichester's to the genius of its medieval masons. Great houses were built here too, with Hampton Court and Hatfield two of the finest buildings from the 1500s and 1600s and then much later the astonishing Brighton Pavilion, built by the Prince Regent in the early nineteenth century. But it is back to London for that most modern of monuments, the London Eye, which anyone can ride in and experience an aerial view for themselves.

HATFIELD HOUSE
Hertfordshire

Hatfield House in Hertfordshire is one of England's most magnificent Jacobean houses. Elizabeth I grew up here in the royal palace. The estate was given by James I to his chief minister Robert, Earl of Salisbury, who demolished most of the palace and built the big house here in 1611. Hatfield remains in the family's hands though it escaped disaster in 1835 when the dowager duchess accidentally started a fire that killed her and destroyed one of the wings. It was later entirely restored.

WINDSOR CASTLE
Berkshire

Windsor Castle towers above the River Thames beside rolling parkland. Its history stretches all the way back to the Norman Conquest of 1066, when William the Conqueror built a keep to guard the western approaches to London. Later kings, especially Edward III and Charles II, enlarged and improved Windsor. Today it survives as not only the largest but also the oldest occupied castle in the world, restored after a major fire in 1992, and is one of the homes of the royal family.

ETON COLLEGE
Berkshire

Eton College, probably the most famous school in the world (and certainly one of the most expensive), is near Windsor in Berkshire. However, its prestige (which includes being able to boast 19 former British prime ministers) ensures there is no shortage of boys wishing to obtain one of the 1,300-odd places. Eton was founded by Henry VI in 1440 and one of its most important buildings is the fifteenth-century chapel, the most prominent building visible here and on the ground.

CITY OF LONDON
London

This is the very centre of the City of London, the traditional 'square mile', still bounded by the remains of the medieval city walls built themselves on top of Roman foundations. Today few people live in the City. This is the United Kingdom's international financial centre and the skyline is dominated by the massive commercial buildings, though here and there amongst them it is easy to pick out the churches built by Sir Christopher Wren after the Great Fire of 1666.

ST PAUL'S CATHEDRAL
London

On Sir Christopher Wren's tomb, deep beneath St Paul's, is a Latin motto: *Si requiris monumentum, circumspice*, meaning 'if you seek his monument, look around'. St Paul's of course was Wren's greatest gift to London. The old medieval cathedral was left in ruins after the Great Fire. Wren produced several controversial designs for a new cathedral and it was several years before the plan was finally agreed. Work was finished in 1709, leaving the result that triumphantly defied the Blitz of 1940–41.

LONDON MARATHON

London

The legend of the marathon dates back to 490 BC when Pheidippides was said to have run from the Battle of Marathon to Athens to announce defeat of the Persians. Today's marathons are set at just over 41 km (26.22 miles). London's marathon was founded in 1981 and takes runners through one of the most stunning running routes in the world, starting at Greenwich in south-east London and ending up near Buckingham Palace. The fastest take just a little over two hours.

TATE MODERN

London

Almost directly opposite St Paul's Cathedral, and joined by the pedestrian Millennium Bridge over the Thames, the Tate Modern gallery is one of the most imaginative uses of an old building in Britain. Once the Bankside Power Station, this vast brick structure has a chimney almost 100 m (328 ft) tall and was finished in 1963. Less than 30 years later it was closed but instead of being demolished, the insides were stripped out and the modern art displays installed, opening to great acclaim in 2000.

LONDON EYE
London

Clinging to the south bank of the Thames, the London Eye has been carrying passengers up to 135 m (443 ft) above the river since 1999. This view is taken from almost at the top looking north-east across the Hungerford Railway Bridge and beyond is Waterloo Bridge. Each circuit of the wheel, the largest of its kind, with its 32 special observation cars takes about half an hour, with passengers hopping on and off as the cars slowly move past the boarding ramp.

HOUSES OF PARLIAMENT
London

The River Thames is the key to London's historical greatness, and there is no more appropriate place than the Palace of Westminster to appreciate that. Charles Barry's magnificent Houses of Parliament, finished in 1852, tower over the river on the north bank though Westminster Hall dates back to 1097. Beyond lie the modern government departments of Whitehall. Tourists today can fly above Parliament themselves by taking a ride on the London Eye, a great rotating wheel with observation cars on the south bank.

RIVER THAMES & BRIDGES
London

As the River Thames flows through London, it heads north past Westminster and then turns sharply to the east to make for the North Sea. This view shows the river with its regular flotilla of sightseeing boats coming up to that bend, flowing past the Houses of Parliament and then under Westminster Bridge. It begins to curve, past the London Eye, to the Hungerford Bridge that carries trains across the river to southern England. Next comes Waterloo Bridge, before it completes its turn and reaches the City of London.

WATERLOO STATION
London

Perhaps it is an irony that this great railway station, named after the Battle of Waterloo in 1815 that saw the end of Napoleon's ambitions, is now where trains leave for France from through the Channel Tunnel. But most of all Waterloo Station is a place where millions of commuters pass through every year on their way to work from the counties south-west of London, while others head for the nearby National Theatre and Royal Festival Hall on the south bank of the Thames.

BUCKINGHAM PALACE

London

The Duke of Buckingham built a house on this site in London in 1703. King George II took it over in 1762 and started the process of transforming it into a palace and creating the wings arranged around a central courtyard. It was not until 1837, when Victoria succeeded as queen, that Buckingham Palace became the official London residence of the monarch. Bombed in 1940, the Palace survived with little damage and remains today one of the most popular tourist destinations in the capital.

HAMPTON COURT

Surrey

Thomas Wolsey, Henry VIII's Archbishop of York, rebuilt Hampton Court in the early 1500s before the King seized the palace. William III and Mary II (1689–94) added a new wing, but were especially keen on the gardens and it was then that the famous maze was planted in its present form (possibly replacing an earlier one). Anyone braving the maze without a map faces half a mile of paths winding throughout the 0.14 ha (⅓ acre) site, famously featured in *Three Men in a Boat* (1889).

CANTERBURY CATHEDRAL
Kent

There is no finer example of the sheer brilliance of the medieval church-builders than Canterbury Cathedral, one of the oldest and most famous Christian buildings in Britain. The seat of the Archbishop of Canterbury, head of the Church of England, the present structure dates back to Archbishop Lanfranc (1070–77) who rebuilt the ruined Saxon building. The most famous event here was the murder of Thomas à Becket in 1170, which turned Canterbury into a special place for pilgrims to his shrine.

LEEDS CASTLE
Kent

Not to be confused with Leeds in Yorkshire, this is Leeds Castle in Kent just a few miles from Maidstone. The present building on the island in the lake dates back to 1119. Six queens lived here, including Catherine of Aragon for whom Henry VIII converted Leeds into a palace. Parliament spared Leeds in the Civil War because the Culpepper family who owned it then were Parliamentarians. Leeds is one of the most popular attractions in south-east England.

BRIGHTON PAVILION
East Sussex

This Regency extravaganza is the Brighton Pavilion, designed by John Nash for George, Prince of Wales, in 1815. During the illness of his father, George III, the prince acted as regent and is known to history as Prince Regent and was extremely interested in art, design and fashion, hence the term 'Regency' being applied to many buildings of this time. The Pavilion is unique in its use of various eastern styles from India, Mongolia and China to create a fantasy retreat for the prince.

BEACHY HEAD
East Sussex

What more evocative sight could there be of England's coast than the white cliffs of the south coast? Beachy Head is the most southerly point of Sussex, just a mile or two from the famous seaside resort of Eastbourne. At 162 m (532 ft), it is Britain's tallest chalk cliff, commanding magnificent views to east and west. Beachy Head has the unenviable reputation as a popular place for suicides. The present lighthouse was built in 1902 to protect shipping, replacing an earlier one built in 1831.

ARUNDEL CASTLE
West Sussex

Visitors to Arundel see the castle from a completely different angle. It towers over the little town beside the crossing of the Arun deep in the heart of West Sussex, and it is impossible to see within. The ancient eleventh-century motte with its twelfth-century keep is easily visible here, but it was the nineteenth-century fascination with all-things medieval that caused Henry Howard, fifteenth Duke of Norfolk, to rebuild Arundel as a huge Gothic castle, now one of the biggest in England.

CHICHESTER CATHEDRAL
West Sussex

This dramatic view shows Chichester Cathedral's west end and soaring spire to excellent effect. Although the church dates back to the late eleventh century and is itself built in the heart of the Roman city of Noviomagus, fires and other problems led to various bouts of rebuilding in succeeding centuries to create a unique combination of styles. The disasters continued to early modern times for the medieval spire, which was repaired in the late 1600s, totally collapsed in 1861 and had to be rebuilt from scratch.

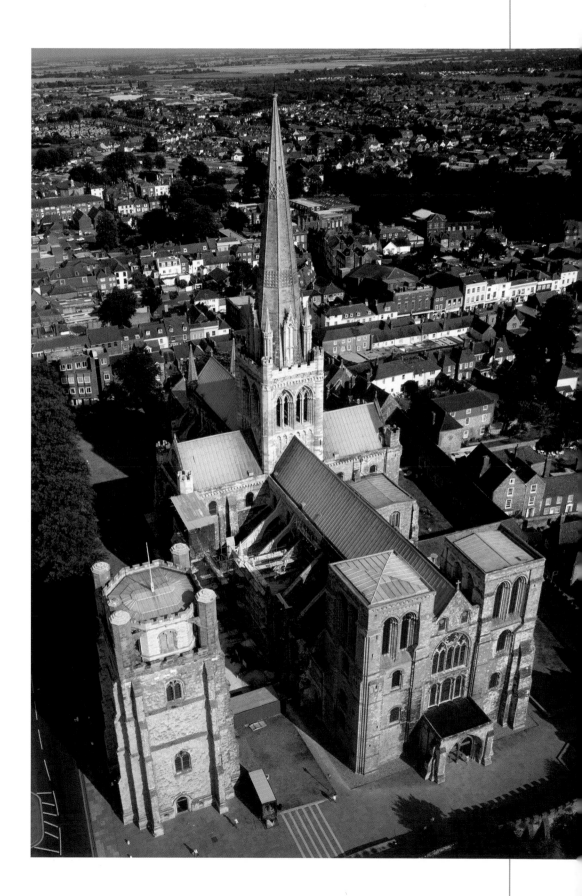

THE NEEDLES
Isle of Wight

The Isle of Wight lies just off the Hampshire coast near Southampton. Famous today for its tourism and the annual Cowes regatta, it has a unique quality as a kind of miniature England. One of the most famous places to visit is the Needles, a series of chalk stacks at the most westerly point of the island, though the needle-shaped stack that gave the formation its name collapsed in 1764. Since 1859 a lighthouse has protected shipping creeping past into Southampton Water.

South-West England

England's south-west stretches from the vast ancient landscape of Salisbury Plain to the turbulent coastline of Cornwall.

The area boasts three of the most important prehistoric monuments in the whole world: Stonehenge, Avebury and Silbury Hill, which all date back to the time when the men and women of the Neolithic Stone Age started to clear the forests in order to farm. By the Middle Ages some parts of this region were wealthy and could afford the stunning cathedral church of Salisbury, one of the most stylistically coherent medieval churches in Europe, as well as the magnificent stately home at Longleat.

The Industrial Revolution brought the railways to this region, and other great achievements like the Clifton Suspension Bridge. But the south-west stretches a long way from here into Cornwall where the land is wilder and remote. The coastline includes Torquay's elegant seafront, the curious formation of Chesil Beach, and an endless parade of rocky cliffs and dramatic views, broken up here and there by fishing villages like Clovelly and Mousehole. Exmoor and Dartmoor are two of the nation's most important national parks and are as popular with holidaymakers and walkers as the coastal sights of Land's End and St Michael's Mount.

CLIFTON SUSPENSION BRIDGE

Bristol

Clifton Suspension Bridge joins Bristol to North Somerset by spanning the Avon Gorge triumphantly. Work started on Isambard Kingdom Brunel's design in 1831 but was unfinished when he died in 1859, delayed by the Bristol riots and money problems. It was only completed in 1864 using chains from Brunel's Hungerford Bridge in London, demolished in 1860, and has remained in use ever since. Famously, in 1885, a lady tried to commit suicide by jumping off, but was saved when her skirts acted as a parachute.

ROYAL CRESCENT
Bath

Bath's fame lies in its celebrated hot water spring. The Romans turned this place into a healing complex, visited by the sick from across the Roman Empire. The remains of their baths and temple are one of Bath's greatest sights. But the glory of Bath today is its streets, squares and houses built with honey-coloured Bath stone, of its Regency heyday when it became the most fashionable place in Georgian England, immortalised by Jane Austen in *Northanger Abbey* (written in 1798).

KENNET AND AVON CANAL
Wiltshire

This is just part of the 140-km (87-mile)-long Kennet and Avon canal which links the rivers Kennet and Thames in the east at Reading to the Avon at Bristol in the west. Construction started in 1794 and took 16 years. This section is the Caen Hill series of 16 locks out of the 29 that make up the Devizes Flight. The canal gradually fell into disuse after the railways arrived but the canal was restored by a dedicated Trust and reopened in 1990.

SILBURY HILL
Wiltshire

From a distance this looks like a Norman castle motte, but Silbury Hill is not only prehistoric in date but also Europe's largest man-made hill. It was begun nearly 5,000 years ago in the Neolithic period by digging out a 250,000 cubic m (326,988 cubic yds) of chalk to create a circular mound that eventually rose to 40 m (131 ft) in height. Despite various excavations, no-one has ever worked out why Silbury Hill was built, though it lies in an area rich in prehistoric monuments.

AVEBURY
Wiltshire

Far bigger than the more famous Stonehenge, the Neolithic henge monument at Avebury is more than 420 m (1,378 ft) wide and dates back some 5,000 years to when the circular ditch and outer mound was dug. Not long afterwards about 98 standing stones were laid out in a circle within the ditch, making the biggest prehistoric stone circle known, with two smaller stone circles within. By the late Middle Ages locals started demolishing the circle for the stone, but these days Avebury is protected.

STONEHENGE
Wiltshire

Photographed at sunset in mid-winter, this is unmistakeably the most famous prehistoric monument in Europe and perhaps the world. Stonehenge was a temple and astronomical instrument built in its present form by 2000 BC in the heart of Salisbury Plain, but started life a thousand years earlier. Some of the stones were brought here from the Presely Mountains in Wales but no-one knows how the ancient peoples did this. Every year pilgrims gather on midsummer's day to greet the sunrise.

SALISBURY & CATHEDRAL
Wiltshire

The local centre was once nearby at Old Sarum but in 1220 the bishopric was moved to Salisbury and a new cathedral was begun. What makes Salisbury extremely unusual is that it was built entirely in the Early English Gothic style and was largely completed by 1280 with the spire finished by 1320. The result was an enormous building with England's highest spire and largest cloisters. The tower is 123 m (404 ft) high, with the colossal downward thrust resisted by massive buttresses.

LONGLEAT
Wiltshire

Today Longleat is best-known for its wildlife safari park and the personality of the current owner Alexander Thynn, the seventh Marquess of Bath. He is a direct descendant of the first owner, Sir John Thynne, who began the house in 1572 following a major fire. Designed to be outward-looking and to combine the French love of symmetry with the English courtyard house, it remains one of the most innovative, best-preserved and complete examples of Elizabethan country house architecture in England.

MAIDEN CASTLE
Dorset

Near Dorchester in Dorset, Maiden Castle dates back around 6,000 years but it was only around 2,500 years ago that the place was developed into the largest Iron Age hillfort in Britain with gigantic fortifications. Many others survive, showing that this was how Britain's ancient tribal leaders showed their power and protected their people. When the Roman army arrived here in the late summer of AD 43 it made short work of the defenders. Archaeologists have found the defenders' skeletons where they fell.

CERNE GIANT
Dorset

Leaving nothing to the imagination and casting modesty aside, the Cerne Abbas Giant is a prehistoric figure cut into the hills of central Dorset. One theory is that he dates back 2,000 years to the Iron Age or possibly even earlier, perhaps representing a warrior fertility god, though the style and the club suggest perhaps a Roman representation of Hercules. But with no record of the figure before the seventeenth century at the earliest, no-one knows, and the Giant is saying nothing.

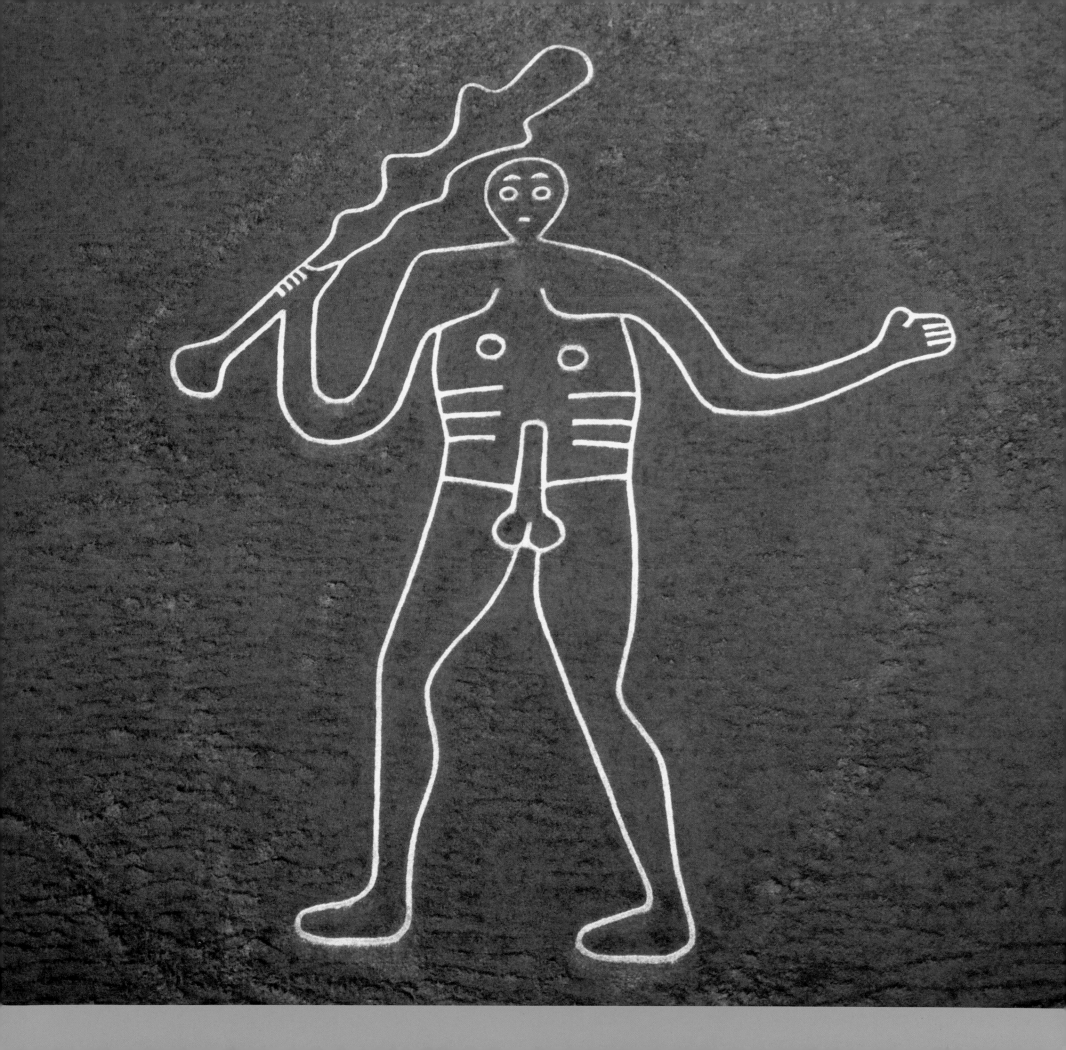

CHESIL BEACH
Dorset

This huge bank of sand and shingle is Chesil Beach in Dorset, which joins the Isle of Portland to the mainland near Weymouth and shelters the coastline from the choppy waters of the English Channel, creating a safe lagoon haven for holidaymakers and small boats. The natural phenomenon is known as a 'tombolo', caused by waves meeting longshore drift and causing sediment to accumulate in one stretch. The result here is 29 km (18 miles) in length and 18 m (59 ft) in height.

CORFE CASTLE
Dorset

One of the most dramatic ruined castles in the British Isles, Corfe was built by the Norman invaders to guard the pass through Dorset's Isle of Purbeck, which overlooks the strategically vital entrance to Poole Harbour. King John (1199–1216) liked Corfe and had the castle enlarged to create something so impregnable that it withstood two sieges in the English Civil War of the 1640s. Efforts to demolish it after the war were abandoned, leaving the stunning ruin clinging to the hill today.

TILLY WHIM CAVES
Dorset

It is hard to believe that this picture has anything to do with St Paul's Cathedral but these limestone quarries on the south-east point of the Isle of Purbeck at Durlston Head produced the stone for the cathedral and many other buildings. The stone was hacked out, creating the caves, and lowered to waiting barges. The coastal quarries have not been worked since the early nineteenth century and are closed to public access for safety reasons. These days Purbeck stone is quarried further inland.

OLD HARRY ROCKS
Dorset

The most easterly point of the Isle of Purbeck is the Foreland. Just below is a series of chalk stacks known as the Old Harry Rocks. The whole area is an extremely dangerous place with sheer cliffs, though a clifftop path does wind its way around the headland from Swanage to Studland. Old Harry was created some two centuries ago when erosion cut him off from the mainland. Beyond him once was 'Old Harry's Wife' but she collapsed many years ago.

GLASTONBURY & TOR
Somerset

Tor is an ancient word that means 'conical hill'. It could not be more apt for this curious piece of high ground in the Somerset Levels, with the tower of the long-vanished St Michael's church on top where the last Abbot of Glastonbury Abbey was hung in 1539 during the Dissolution of the Monasteries. The terraced sides were created by medieval farmers, and archaeology has shown that Glastonbury was home to a prehistoric lakeside village long before when the levels were flooded.

EXMOOR
Devon/Somerset

Exmoor hugs Devon and Somerset's north coast and is where the River Exe rises to flow south across the county to Exeter, helped by the heavy rainfall that sometimes exceeds 2 m (80 in) a year. The view is west to Foreland Point in the distance past hills that rise over 400 m (1,312 ft) above the shore, and many of the clifftops themselves are still more than 200 m (656 ft) high. There are many areas of distinctive coastal woodland, some of which can be seen here.

CLOVELLY
Devon

Tiny Clovelly village is tightly packed into a narrow valley on Devon's north coast at the top of a 122-m (400-ft)-high cliff in Bideford Bay. No cars are allowed here, and visitors must make their way through the cobbled streets on foot. Although today the village depends on tourism, it still looks very much as it did when the main activity was herring fishing in the eighteenth century.

DARTMOOR
Devon

Dartmoor National Park occupies a large part of south Devon to the west of Exeter, covering around 958 sq km (370 sq miles). Its distinctive appearance is the result of weathering which has exposed the hard granite hilltops known as 'tors'. It is an extremely popular place for walking and camping, and is still also used for military training. But Dartmoor can also be dangerous and bleak, the cause of many legends due in no small part to the prehistoric monuments scattered across its hills.

TORQUAY
Devon

Bathed in the mild air flowing across the Atlantic Ocean, Torquay on Devon's south coast enjoys one of the pleasantest climates in the British Isles. No wonder it has been a fashionable resort for a very long time, mainly since the days of the Napoleonic Wars when those desperate for a healthy climate, or rich English families in search of a Riviera holiday, had to look closer to home. This view is Hope's Nose, a promontory on the south side of Babbacombe Bay.

TINTAGEL
Cornwall

This is all that remains of the Great Hall of Tintagel Castle, which clings to a rocky headland on the north coast of Cornwall. A bleak and romantic setting, often lashed by Atlantic storms, Tintagel has a truly ancient history that goes back to the days of the Roman Empire and beyond. Its fame comes from its mythical association with the legend of King Arthur, but the ruins mostly belong to the time of Richard, Earl of Cornwall, in the thirteenth century.

EDEN PROJECT
Cornwall

From up here the Eden Project, near St Austell in Cornwall, looks like a giant grub emerging from the soil. In reality this is a major experiment built in an old china clay quarry. Eden is designed to recreate a tropical environment in one dome, and a Mediterranean environment in the other, to see how animals and plants adapt themselves to the local soil and environmental conditions. Although Eden is now a major visitor attraction it is also dedicated to education.

THE LIZARD

Cornwall

Lizard Point is the most southerly part of Cornwall, and therefore the whole British Isles. A vital landmark in the days when navigation relied on the sun and stars, mariners headed for home from voyages to the Mediterranean or across the Atlantic knew that once they saw the Lizard then Plymouth or Portsmouth were within reach. But the Lizard was also extremely dangerous and hundreds of ships whose captains miscalculated were wrecked on the rocky coast.

ST IVES

Cornwall

There are three St Ives in England, and this is Cornwall's. The view here is of 'The Island', a peninsula jutting out from the main town into St Ives Bay on the north Cornish coast. The huge sandy beach means it is hardly necessary to say this is a popular holiday destination, a habit the Victorians started in the late 1870s when the railway, which still runs here, was built. It meant an end to St Ives' dependence on the fishing industry.

ST MICHAEL'S MOUNT

Cornwall

Our aerial vantage point takes us out to sea here, high above Mount's Bay in Cornwall and above St Michael's Mount close to Penzance. The natural causeway from Marazion some 400 m (1,312 ft) away on the mainland is submerged during high tide, making this a tidal island. St Michael's church dates back to the fifteenth century, since when it has played an important role as a landmark for shipping, some of which makes its way into the small harbour on the north side.

MOUSEHOLE

Cornwall

Mousehole lies on the west side of Mount's Bay in Cornwall. These days Mousehole is a small place, mainly concerned with the tourist trade. But once it was an important port on the Cornish coast, indeed important enough for the Spanish to attack Mousehole in 1595 and raze it to the ground. Since those times, other places like nearby Penzance and Newlyn have grown much larger but Mousehole is famous for its beautiful harbour, seen to its best advantage from this overhead view.

LAND'S END

Cornwall

The name says it all. Here we are facing due west looking out over Land's End towards the lighthouse on the Longships Rocks a mile or so out to sea and the Scilly Isles beyond. This is not the most westerly point of Britain (parts of Scotland beat it), but it makes no difference to the thousands of people who make their way across Cornwall to the far end of the Penwith peninsula, and those who start their treks to John O' Groats from here.

Index